Living Nature

AMPHIBIANS

Chrysalis Children's Books

The publishers wish to thank the following for permission to reproduce copyright material:

Oxford Scientific Films and individual copyright holders on the following pages: Kathie Atkinson 7 top; G I Bernard 8 bottom, 23, 24; Mike Birkhead 27 right; Martin Chillmaid 5 bottom; J A L Cooke 16 top, 19 bottom; Jack Dermid 3, 21 left; Michael Fogden 9 both, 13, 18, 25 top, 28/29; Paul Franklin 4 right, 7 bottom left; Jim Frazier/Mantis Wildlife Films 27 left; Breck P Kent/Animals Animals 8 top, 25 bottom; R K La Val/Animals Animals 4 left; Michael Leach 11 bottom, 20 top; Zig Leszczynski/Animals Animals cover, 1, 6, 7 centre right, 11 top, 19 top, 20 bottom, 21 right, 22; Mike Linley 5 top, 10, 12; Stan Osolinski 26; Avril Ramage 17; Alastair Shay 16 bottom.

This edition published in 2003 by

Chrysalis Children's Books
The Chrysalis Building, Bramley Rd,
London W10 6SP

Text copyright © Angela Royston
Photographs copyright © Oxford Scientific Films and individual copyright holders
Format and illustrations © Chrysalis Books PLC

Printed in Hong Kong

ISBN 1 84138 627 8

British Library Cataloguing in Publication Data
CIP data for this book is available from the British Library

A Belitha Book

Editor: Veronica Ross
Designers: Frances McKay and James Lawrence
Consultant: Steve Pollock

Words in **bold** are in the glossary on page 30.

Title page picture:
A Colorado River toad from the USA.

Contents page picture:
A cave salamander.

Contents

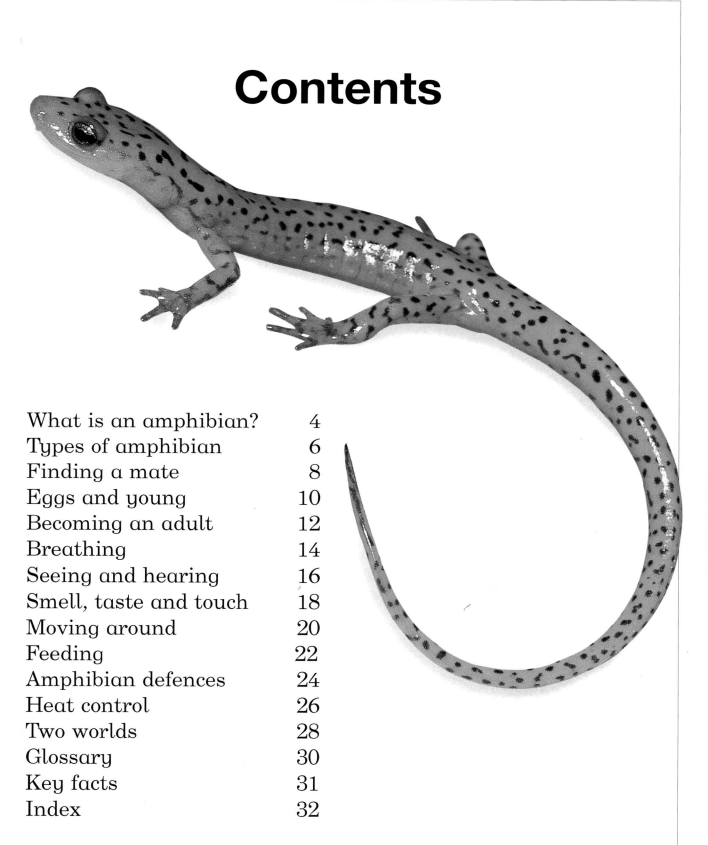

What is an amphibian?

The animals shown here are all amphibians. They come from different parts of the world. Amphibians are animals that spend part of their lives in water and part of their lives on land.

▼ This is a crested **newt** from Europe. The crest, which is on the newt's back, looks like a fin.

▲ This emerald glass frog comes from the forests of Central America.

Most amphibians begin life as an egg, which is laid in water. **Tadpoles** hatch from the eggs. A newly-hatched tadpole has a head, body and a tail.

The tadpoles grow four legs, and change into adults. The adults live on land, but they stay near water because they need to keep their skin damp.

▲ This is a fire **salamander**. Most salamanders are brightly coloured.

▲ This is a natterjack toad. Toads look very similar to frogs.

Types of amphibian

There are three different kinds of amphibian. Adult frogs and toads have four legs but no tail. Their back legs are very strong which makes them good at jumping. Toads spend more time on land than frogs and often have a thicker skin.

Salamanders and newts have four legs and a long tail. Some kinds of salamander live all their lives in water. Others live in trees, and some burrow under the ground.

▼ This northern red salamander looks for food on the stony bed of a stream.

▲ This cane toad is so large it can swallow a whole pygmy possum.

▶ Caecilians look like worms, but they are amphibians.

A tiny tree frog on a toadstool.

Caecilians have long bodies, short tails and no legs. They burrow underground in damp soil like worms. They have strong, bony heads to push their way through the soil.

Finding a mate

Many amphibians return to the pond or stream where they were born in order to find a **mate**. Amphibians must find a mate before they can have young.

Male frogs and toads croak and shout to attract females. They puff out their throats to make their calls louder. The females, fat with eggs, hop towards the males.

◄ Two American toads mating in a pond.

▼ This male newt dances to attract a mate.

When the female frog has chosen a mate, the male climbs on to her back and they swim together. As she lays her eggs in the water, the male covers them with a milky fluid to **fertilize** them.

Some salamanders and newts don't lay eggs. The young develop inside the female's body.

▲ A male frog calling for a mate.

These male frogs are fighting to win a female.

Eggs and young

Most amphibians lay thousands of eggs. Each egg is covered with sticky jelly and all the eggs float together in water. Some amphibians take no notice of the eggs once they are laid. Many eggs are eaten by fish and other animals.

Other amphibians lay fewer eggs and take great care of them. One kind of male frog carries the eggs in a pouch in his throat. When the eggs hatch, the young swim out of his mouth! The young that hatch from the eggs are called **larvae**.

◄ The male midwife toad carries the eggs around with him until they are ready to hatch.

◄ A marbled salamander guards her eggs by curling her body and tail around them.

The larvae of frogs and toads are called tadpoles. Tadpoles have no legs and breathe through **gills** on the outside of their bodies.

Did you know?

Robber frogs lay their eggs on land instead of in water. The eggs do not hatch into tadpoles, instead tiny frogs crawl out.

◄ A young tadpole has feathery gills which help it breathe under water.

Becoming an adult

When they first hatch, young amphibians have gills and take in **oxygen** from the water. When they begin to change into adults, they grow **lungs** inside their bodies and their gills close up. Then the amphibians must swim to the surface of the water to breathe in air. At the same time they begin to grow legs and feet.

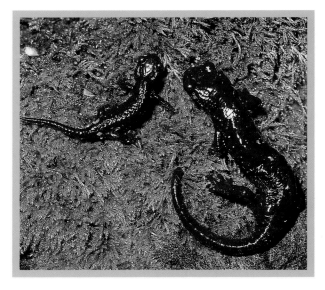

▲ Alpine salamanders do not lay eggs. They give birth to young that look like small adults.

▼ A tadpole slowly changes into a frog. The back legs grow, then the front legs. The tail gets shorter.

frog spawn

young tadpole

fully-grown tadpole

back legs grow

front legs grow

◀ Axolotls are a kind of salamander that never change into an adult. They keep their gills and they spend all their time in water.

Frogs grow back legs first and then their tails disappear. Salamanders and newts grow front legs first, and caecilians never grow legs at all.

A fully-grown frog on land.

young frog with shorter tail

Breathing

All animals need oxygen to stay alive. Both water and air contain oxygen, but amphibians are the only animals that can breathe in air and water.

Adult amphibians have simple lungs. They are two thin bags lined with tiny **blood vessels**. Oxygen passes through the lungs into the blood vessels.

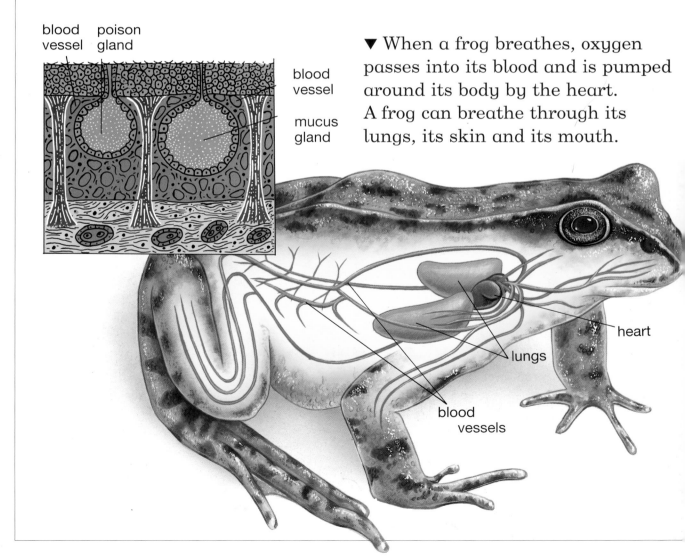

blood vessel   poison gland

blood vessel

mucus gland

▼ When a frog breathes, oxygen passes into its blood and is pumped around its body by the heart. A frog can breathe through its lungs, its skin and its mouth.

heart

lungs

blood vessels

Amphibians can also breathe through the damp lining of their mouths and through their skin. Their skin is thin and covered with a slimy fluid called mucus, which oxygen can pass through easily.

The mucus is made in **glands** in the skin, just as glands in human skin make sweat. Some amphibians have glands that make poison. The poison protects them from attack (see page 25).

▼ Gills work like lungs. As water flows over the gills, oxygen passes into the blood.

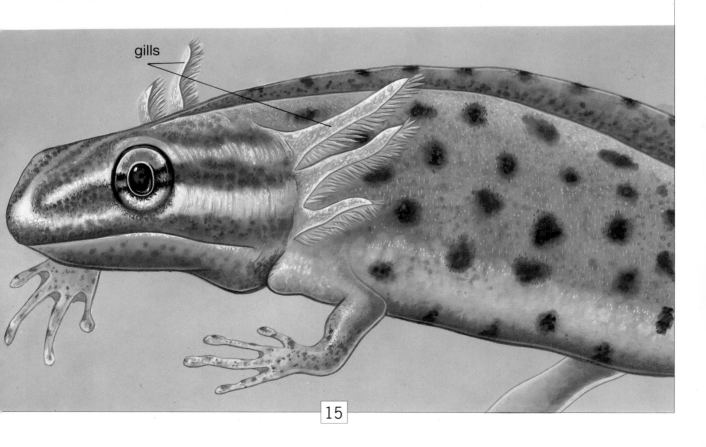

gills

Seeing and hearing

Most amphibians have good eyesight, except for caecilians which cannot see very well at all.

Frogs and salamanders have the best eyesight. Frogs and toads have eyes on the top of their head, so they can see all around.

Frogs are very good at seeing things that move. They quickly snap up insects that fly by.

▲ Caecilians are nearly blind.

A frog's ears are just behind its eyes.

All amphibians can hear, but frogs and toads hear best. They can hear just as well in water as they can in air. They listen out for danger and for each other's calls.

Frogs and toads have lots of calls. Males have one call to attract a mate, one to warn off rivals, and one to warn others of danger. Frogs have a special croak for when it rains!

▼ This frog's body is well hidden in the water while its big eyes look all around.

Did you know?

A frog only notices things that move. It will miss an insect that stays very still.

Smell, taste and touch

Amphibians smell with their nostrils, like we do. Caecilians use smell to find food. Newts become so excited when they smell food, they attack any other newt that comes near.

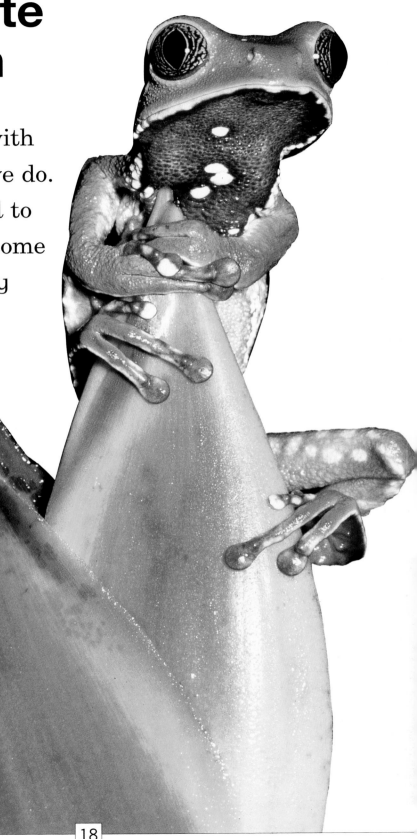

▶ This leaf frog has a good view from the top of a plant, but it also uses its sense of smell to find out what is going on.

The sense of taste is important to amphibians. Many insects taste nasty which stops other animals eating them. Amphibians taste with their tongues, as we do. If a toad catches an insect that tastes nasty, it will quickly spit the insect out. It will only eat it if it tastes good.

▲ This toad cannot see much in the murky water, but it can tell if something is moving nearby.

▼ This toad is about to catch an insect. If it tastes good, the toad will swallow it. If it tastes bad, the toad will spit it out.

Amphibians use their sense of touch to tell them when other animals are nearby. They can feel tiny movements in the water or in the ground.

Did you know?

We may feel the ground shake when a heavy lorry passes by. A frog feels the ground shake when another frog passes by!

Moving around

▼ A frog uses its long back legs to leap from leaf to leaf across a pond.

Amphibians move about in different ways. They swim, jump, crawl, and some can even glide.

Frogs and toads can move fast in water and on land. They have long back legs with **webbed feet**. They use their feet like flippers to swim through the water. Toads hop or walk along the ground, but frogs take huge jumps. They bend their back legs and push down hard on the ground. Then they leap up and forward.

▲ This toad has webbed feet and a claw on its back foot for digging.

Some tree frogs can glide a short distance through the air. Their webbed feet slow down their fall.

Newts and salamanders swim through water by wriggling their backs from side to side, like a fish.

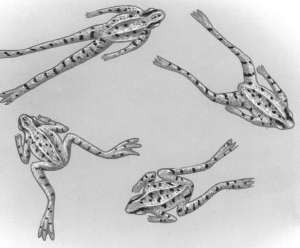

▲ Frogs use their strong back legs and webbed feet to push them through the water.

Salamanders bend their bodies into an S-shape when they walk. This lets them take longer steps.

▲ Salamanders wiggle their bodies from side to side as they walk.

► This tree frog uses its webbed feet like wings to glide through the air.

Feeding

Most amphibians eat other animals. Frogs and toads feed on insects, snails and larvae. Some frogs and toads catch small birds, fish and mammals.

Many frogs and toads catch **prey** with their long, sticky tongues, which they can flick in and out of their mouths very quickly.

A tree frog catching an insect.

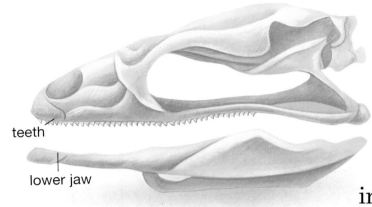

teeth

lower jaw

◄ Amphibians have teeth. They use them to grip their food not to chew it.

Most salamanders and newts feed on insects, worms, slugs and other similar small animals. Some kinds of salamanders have tongues as long as their bodies.

Frogs that feed in water gulp their prey into their mouths. Tadpoles nibble plants and insect larvae.

► Frogs and toads use their eyes to help them swallow. Their eyes sink into their heads, pushing the food down their throats.

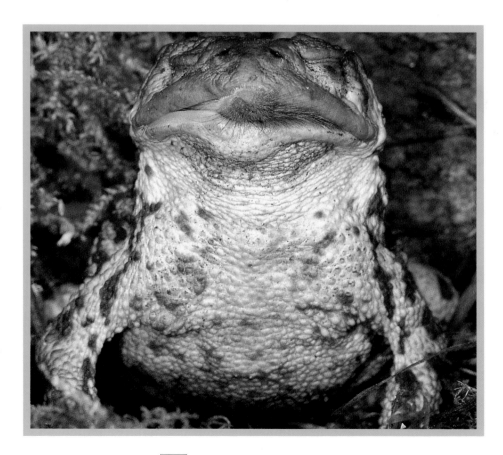

Amphibian defences

Amphibians are hunted by **mammals**, birds and **reptiles**. Amphibians do not have sharp teeth or claws to defend themselves. Instead they try to avoid attack by not being seen. Some hide by blending in with their surroundings and staying very still.

▶ This little tree frog is hard to see because it is the same colour as the leaves it is hiding among.

Other amphibians are brightly coloured. The colours warn other animals that their skin contains poison. Some frogs are so poisonous they kill any animal that eats them.

Many frogs and toads blow themselves up with air to make themselves look bigger. This makes them hard to swallow.

▲ The poison from this arrow-poison frog is so deadly people use it to make poison arrows.

If a salamander is caught by the tail, its tail breaks off and a new one grows.

▶ The slimy salamander is covered with a sticky slime that gets up the nose of any animal that attacks it.

Heat control

Amphibians have to keep warm to keep active. But they cannot make their own heat. Instead they have to get their heat from their surroundings.

▶ This American toad is warming up in the sun while it sits on the back of a turtle.

Amphibians sit in the sun to warm up. When they are warm enough they move into the shade. An amphibian must not let its skin dry out. If its skin does become dry, the amphibian cools down. The colder it is, the slower it becomes.

In some countries the winter is so cold that an amphibian goes into a kind of deep sleep, called **hibernation**. Its heart slows down and its body becomes cold. Before it hibernates, it finds a safe, damp place to hide at the bottom of a pond.

▼ This Australian burrowing frog has a waterproof skin to stop it drying out.

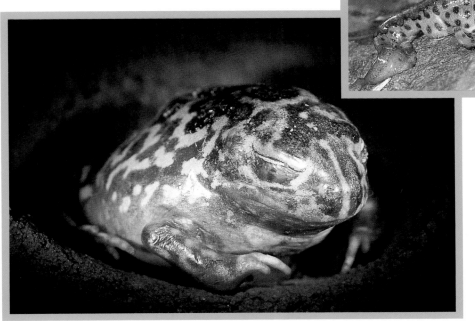

▲ This newt hunts at night so that its damp skin does not dry out in the heat of the sun.

Two worlds

These gleaming golden toads are from Central America.

There are over 2000 kinds of amphibian. Many live in rainforests and grassy meadows. Some live in deserts, but none live in the sea or at the icy North and South Poles.

Wherever they live, amphibians spend their lives in two worlds – in water and on land. The word amphibian means 'both lives'. But there are exceptions.

Some salamanders live their whole lives in water, and some toads give birth to little toads rather than laying eggs. But all amphibians have a thin, moist skin.

Glossary

Blood vessels The network of tubes that carry blood around the body.

Caecilian A kind of amphibian which has no legs and lives under the ground.

Fertilize To join together male and female cells to have young.

Gills Part of an amphibian's body used for breathing. In the gills, oxygen passes from water into the blood.

Gland Part of the body that produces a special substance. An amphibian's mucus glands help keep its skin moist.

Hibernation A sleep-like state that some animals fall into to survive harsh winter weather.

Larvae Young newts and salamanders before they have changed into adults. Young insects are also called larvae.

Lungs Parts of the body used for breathing in air.

Mammals The group of animals that have fur or hair and feed their young with their own milk.

Mate One of a pair of animals (one male and one female) who together have young.

Newts A kind of amphibian which has four legs and a tail when it is an adult.

Oxygen A gas which all living things need to stay alive. Air and water contain oxygen.

Prey An animal that is hunted for food by another animal.

Pygmy possum A small mammal that lives in Australasia.

Reptiles A group of animals with cold blood and dry, scaly skin.

Salamander A kind of amphibian that has four legs and a tail when it is an adult.

Tadpole A young frog or toad.

Webbed feet Feet with the toes joined by a layer of skin.

Key facts

Largest amphibian The giant salamander which lives in China and Japan grows up to 1.5 metres long.

Largest frog The goliath frog comes from tropical Africa. The largest one found was nearly 37 centimetres long. When it stretched its legs, it was almost twice as long.

Smallest frog When frogs first jump on to land they are no bigger than your thumb nail. The smallest fully-grown frog is about a centimetre long.

Longest jumper Frogs can jump over 3 metres. If you could jump as well as a frog, you could leap 100 metres – that's the length of a football pitch!

Most eggs Frogs and toads lay thousands of eggs. Giant toads usually lay about 35 000 eggs. Only a few of the eggs survive to grow into adults. Fish, birds and other animals feed on the rest.

Stickiest feet Tree frogs have sticky pads under their feet to help them climb up vines and stems. Their feet are so sticky that tree frogs can climb up a smooth pane of glass.

Most poisonous frog The golden arrow-poison frogs from western Colombia each produce enough poison to kill 1500 people. The local people use the poison to make deadly darts.

Longest hibernation When amphibians hibernate their bodies become very cold. Some survive even if half of their body freezes solid. Russian scientists once found a salamander that had been frozen for 90 years. When they warmed it up, it woke up!

Largest toad Cane toads from South America are the largest toads. They are about the same size as goliath frogs.

Longest-lived amphibian In Japan, many giant salamanders kept as pets and in zoos have lived up to 60 years.

Index